THE HATCHECK GIRL

The Hatcheck Girl

POEMS

∾

Tony Whedon

GREEN WRITERS PRESS   *Brattleboro, Vermont*

Printed in the United States

10 9 8 7 6 5 4 3 2 1

Green Writers Press is a Vermont-based publisher whose mission
is to spread a message of hope and renewal through the words and
images we publish. Throughout we will adhere to our commitment
to preserving and protecting the natural resources of the earth.
To that end, a percentage of our proceeds will be donated to
environmental activist groups like 350.org. Green Writers Press
gratefully acknowledges support from Sundog Poetry Center.

Giving Voice to Writers & Artists
Who Will Make the World a Better Place
www.greenwriterspress.com

Poetry Center

Sundog Poetry Center
www.sundogpoetry.org

ISBN: 978-0997452839

Watercolors by the author.

Visit the author's website for more information and music:
www.tonywhedon.com

PRINTED ON PAPER WITH PULP THAT COMES FROM FSC–CERTIFIED FORESTS, MANAGED FORESTS THAT
GUARANTEE RESPONSIBLE ENVIRONMENTAL, SOCIAL, AND ECONOMIC PRACTICES BY LIGHTNING SOURCE ALL
WOOD PRODUCT COMPONENTS USED IN BLACK & WHITE, STANDARD COLOR, OR SELECT COLOR PAPERBACK
BOOKS, UTILIZING EITHER CREAM OR WHITE BOOKBLOCK PAPER, THAT ARE MANUFACTURED IN THE LAVERGNE,
TENNESSEE PRODUCTION CENTER RE SUSTAINABLE FORESTRY INITIATIVE® (SFI®) CERTIFIED SOURCING

ACKNOWLEDGMENTS

Some of these poems appeared or are forthcoming in:
Alaska Quarterly Review, Antioch Review, Atticus Review, Brilliant Corners, Caribbean Review, Crab Orchard Review, Columbia Review, Dukhoul (India), Harpur Palate, The Hampden-Sydney Poetry Review, New Orleans Review, Ploughshares, Prairie Schooner, Superstition Review, and elsewhere.

Great thanks to musicians Tom Fay, Mike Martello, Will Patton, Tiffany Pfieffer, Barry Ries and Dan Silverman, and to poets Sasha Feinstein, Robert Hahn, Kenneth Rosen, Neil Shepard, Betsy Sholl and David Wojahn for hearing me out and reading my stuff; and to Tamra Higgins and Mary Jane Dickerson of Sundog Poetry, and Dede Cummings of Green Writers Press who welcomed my poems and paintings into this book. And as always to Suzanne Whedon for keeping the light on and waiting up for me.

Contents

❧

III

IV

I

THE TRADITION OF THE NEW

Try to make it new, goddamn it, over and over,
some kind of jazzed up non-sequential fuckup

spaced between the words. Charm it the hell up
with lower case half-tones & write or play it like

it was done how many times before; then
recite it blasé to the woman who loves your stuff because

she don't understand it; play the post-Modern malaise
and spend the first set of your gig blowing spit

out of your horn. Worship the twelve-tone, screw up the
lineation & when that's done, recite the last lines

of "Sonnet 73" to show how to scan a line; make love
to your wife like she's the only one you'll ever love on earth

like she knows she is & after she's tucked in for the night,
go back on the stand & pretend you know what

you're doing though that isn't true. Grin your fabulous grin, launch
yourself into a tune you'll forget when the last reel

to this movie's over. We all rise & tremble in a terrible light.
We go to our graves, a whispered phrase on our lips,

our primary affection still the primary one, the woman
we thought we loved still as lovely as the tunes

we played, the thigh we caress in the vintage light of old age.
You see through it all, don't you? Steer past the blues, the heartbreak,

smell the sweet broom & oleander rising above Cathead Creek.
Evening now—the wind smells like it did when the slave ships

disembarked three centuries ago with this new music.
Lean back and listen to the rumble of the approaching storm.

ON AND ON (AND OFF AGAIN)

I put my horn down as the bass player completes
      his chorus & wait for a last cadenza
that never comes. It's all stopped in mid-motion
      & goes on & on, the tenor clicking his keys,
the drummer goosing his foot cymbal.
Someone in the parking lot's sniffing plastics.
      Someone's in mid-kiss smoothing out
her yellow dress. The tune we're playing
      carries us back to a greener time when
dreams were heartbreak, when words mattered:
I woke to a note on my pillow.
      "Play 'I Should Care,'" it says. "Play
'Oh look at Me Now.'" The tenor picks up
      where I left off, drifting into something
so sweet the girl in the yellow dress quits crying.
I like to think these thoughts that fail to make it
      from my mouthpiece to the bell of my horn
have to do with wisdom; but I'm dripping sweat,
      I'm awash with hard-to-live-by illusions.
Most of us flame out before fifty,
no faltering last chorus, no fading like smoke
      into a photograph from another century to mark
our passing. The lucky ones muster a lick
      or two before the notes they play turn to dust.

MALIBU

For Joss Whedon

I stayed that month with a cousin who wrote
for television. A big yellow house with
a guard dog that never stopped barking.
It's the blue I remember, an oil-slick blue
& its darkening shadow on the quasi-horizon.
I was done with endless suffering: I'd
played so many years my rotator cuff
refused to heal. But I loved looking down
across a rooftop of palms to the swimmers
diving off the jetty. Success was a dying
cloud drifting east, resisting the gravity
& light that tether us to earth. I'd lived
in my cousin's shadow so many years
I wanted part of the action—a TV musical, a
permanent gig in a Late Night band.
Evening stars give way to a midnight moon.
Meanwhile, the dog whose name I forget
won't stop barking. I've locked out
my cousin, I hear him knocking at the door.

Listening to Coyotes at Dusk

A critter opens his yeller mouth and croons
and his companions chime in, one yip and then a yowl,
then the drawn out lunacy
of the hunt down in the ravine below our house.
Good Jesus,

                        give us the sense not to run after them in our own folly,
give us the stamina to stay low-key and musical,
each lazy note trailing the other like hillbilly voices on the radio.

Moon gone down and already a sprinkling of stars
giving way to an army of stars.
The world is a great demon wheel, and the howls and yaps
                        in the night are the teeth of that wheel.
If you stand here long enough you'll learn to hear where
one howl ends and another rises up saying I'm hungry, too.

NOCTURNE FOR TWO HANDS

I'm a fool for beauty

I'd been listening to Phineas Newborn, darkest of jazz
pianists, listening to his blockbuster hands descend in octaves
that nearly put him back in the madhouse where
what he recalled was a blue streak of noise that turned time
into a slow-running Styx so thick with petrochemicals
it burbled its own toxic music,

Newborn, playing Black Coffee,
filling my house with teeth-shattering diatonics,
his fingers faster than Tatum's, his soul blacker than
Strayhorn's. The music stopped and a chill

came into the room. I played the cd again,
turning it up loud. What happened to Phineas Newborn?
He had the same nervous breakdown
over and over till he got it right. He kept smashing his hands
to reach past the beauty that dogged him all his life.

October Moon

Past eleven and no thoughts were left, no lines bled
from the book I'd picked up after ten years believing
I'd made big changes in my life. A pair of mallards

flapped over the observatory, an October moon
glaring down, and I settled into the life awaiting me,
a little late-night piano music, a walk in the dark, no maps

of the world below, not a single evening star.
I reopened the book: Tu Fu was still sick
with fever, his wife and little son in Chang'an

awaiting his return. That old man, just bones and rags,
what sort of genius could he squeeze from
his poor universe? He lived a pitiful life, shitting

his brains out on a river raft home: At a bend
in the river, hills rushed by like wild horses,
a collision of earth and sky, and through blooming

plum trees a path angled back and forth toward
the water. White clouds drifted above a boulder-
strewn valley, crickets went silent. War drums

sounded closer now, the imperial army just days away.

Stop Time

The stars are out,
their time signatures
writ large in the firmament,
and I'm happy with the lies
I tell myself, what they
used to call white lies,
the kind people tell you
when they send you
back to the gospel to
get it right. I've never felt
so goddamn good:
to the east a Chinoiserie
of night-lit clouds jangles
like spare change in my head,
and on the town dock
two good-old country boys
in slouchy hats sing
a blues so low and growly
they crowd out the night.
The stars have convened
to tell me their song's pointless
that time as I know it is relative,
and down Jackson Street I go,
awash in the lies I tell myself
till I get them right.

OUT OF THIS WORLD

I sat there awhile, nobody
but me and my wristwatch
listening, and as I waited
for the final chord to descend,
a moth lit on the rim of my glass,
its blue wings trembling.
I wanted harmony, not
cacophony, I wanted pastels
over the muddy half-tones
of a botched twilight;
I played the record
again and heard Miles
consider how to re-enter
the tune, the moment brought
to a dead stop only to
begin again. Fuck the short
form and its abbreviated joys,
and fuck the spaces
between the notes that
define him—the long ash
of a cigar, diminished,
the grapes planted years ago
that refuse to ripen. Almost
evening in California, a stellar jay
worries at an empty feeder;
the sun slips behind
the hills, and the mountains
darken as night comes on.
I put the record on again,
and when Miles plays
that phrase I swear I hear
the moth's heart
beating helplessly
as it falls into my drink
out of this world.

NEW YEAR'S DAY, 2016

It's a rainy New Year's
too wet outside to take a walk, and too

late in my life to begin
a career as a Sunday painter

      but the little town Suzanne and I've moved to
is rife with them,

        they set up their easels along the US 17 bridge

and paint this-and-that floating seaward.

Rain falling in a great, grand sweep across the river,
the new world stomped and dripped on

      like a Jackson Pollock painting.

Pollock began as a figurative painter
but see what happened to him?

I once liked that he hung out at the Cedar Bar and drank
with The New York poets,

that he killed himself driving drunk, how romantic.

      A smudge of purple marsh grass,

the color of year-end sadness held over, stomped on too,
the day worried and already tarnished

though barely begun.

PLAINSONG

He drove all that day from Richmond down US 17,
the radio on, the cab of his truck thick
              with cigar smoke—cough-cough—
a man of seventy-five in the prime of his dotage
redolent of diesel stink. Before his gig
he ate some fries at B&J's where he'd play that night:
evening was coming on, the harbor lights were bright against
the Low Country sky, and big black men like him
              were loading crates of squid and jelly fish
onto a ship with *Shanghai* on its bow. Worn out
beyond description, born along by forces
that pulled him down the curve of the earth north to south,
he reminded himself how he'd lived moment to moment
in an abandoned houseboat, slapping mosquitoes,
              picky about where & what he played.
Back at B&J's now, not much was expected of him,
old and beat-up as he was. When he lay down
a fistful of chords, the near-empty
room didn't get quiet until he opened his tired,
broken mouth and commenced to sing.

I Love Living in the South

"If you're not going to do anything about it,
get your nose out of all that mess," my mother
used to say. With that thought in mind,
I'm out of the house and down two blocks
to B&J's for breakfast. I like to watch
the locals heap on the grits and bacon,
to hear the help singing from the kitchen.
"No sleep last night," I hear an old white lady say,
"and when I do, I dream of the Devil."
My mother would call this "a privileged
Spiritual Moment." I love the South,
like she does, with all its appendages,
there's so many churches, even the car washes
and gas stations have churchy names—
Jeremiah's Redeemed Auto-Cleansing,
Divine Justice Oil and Lube, and so on—
but to call that lady's joke "spiritual"
is like saying all the suffering in our world
is heaven-sent. I watch customers come
and go. I dig in to the fatty portions
as a man's pain-filled voice rises in the kitchen.
"Man, that IS hot!" and out again
into the weather, I breathe in the low-
octane stink, I head down to the river.
A couple of kids are whooping it up
under the viaduct, a pelican lights
on a piling and is lost in reverie.
At my age I need to pay attention
to weather—weeds and wildflowers
on a riverbank, a poem I threw away
days ago that was beyond saving.

Tufts of coastal cloud promise a day
of rain. The Greeks called this *ekstasis*,
to stand outside yourself and watch
the demon world pass by.

GALLERY

Mid-August and I'm down from Vermont,
bivouacked in my sister's West 80th Street apartment

waiting for the phone to ring when it does and her thin,
                broken voice comes on the line:

"Get here, quick," she says, "It might be today, I feel it coming,"
and I pull the disparate parts of myself together while she goes on

about how it's near-impossible to walk—

"It's a waddle rather than a walk," she quips—and how much
she'd like— "could you manage a bottle of gin

              because it's the last day of my life, ha-ha,"

then she's off the line, and I'm out the door, procrastinating.

At noon on Amsterdam and West 80th the winos are already out
whooping it up.

              I make my way past them to a locksmith where I ask

the little Dominican to replace my sister's lock broken for months!—
and on rainy Broadway I pick up a *Times*

and glance at the headlines TOP SECURITY MEASURES
TAKEN FOR CONVENTION

and pay for the paper and walk three blocks

to the Museum of Natural History and catch
the crosstown to Lenox Hill Hospital.

Missing my stop, I let the bus carry me all the way to the East River.
The rain's stopped, a blessed wind ruffles the roiling waters,

and I find myself genuflecting before a statue of Fiorello LaGuardia
who—in my vexed state—looks like Francis of Assisi.

I've prayed to other secular saints—LBJ,
despite his Vietnam mistake,

and Eleanor Roosevelt, who led a spotless life far as I can tell—
but nobody in my family's talked about death.

        I have the utmost respect for death

now that my mother and father
(and soon my sister) have died of it.

Why not remark on death like one talks about weather?—
it was a partly to mostly cloudy death, a cold front moving through—

why not wear it a bit more lightly?

I hear her voice, first a quarter and then

        a half note, smooth as the wind caroming

down the East River, each note a presentiment
of what I forgot I heard before, not music now, but

the thought of it melting into

        the wake of her passing.

I don't take the bus back to Lenox Hill, but transit on foot
five gilt-encrusted Upper East Side blocks, past trust fund kids

on their little scooters and over-taxed dog walkers to a Zybar's:
on D.'s insistence, with the help of a reed-thin
sub-continental girl, I mix my sister's "green drink"—

        elm bark tea, ground-up mustard greens,
        guava and cumquat juice—a placebo that won't

hasten or postpone anyone's death.

Where's the climactic cry of despairing love,
the Wagnerian finale, the deafening silence?

One after another her husbands and lovers left her—.

        But there was no curtain call, just a spattering
of applause from the gallery.

It's past eleven and Lenox Hill's a dread-provoking two blocks away.

According to the nurses D.'s had no guests—no Lincoln Center
mucky-mucks, no son or daughter heard from since

        my niece last posted she'd taken up scuba diving.

What lasts is D.'s broken voice,
I heard it just yesterday—

"You see, I still can sing, remember me?"
She was Papagena in *The Magic Flute.*

        Now she can't quite crack high C,

but in greener days, she sang like no one but herself.
She took her cue from scratchy LP's and 45's:

in her little attic room, she played "Brigadoon" and "The Nutcracker"
over and over, and we thought of her as a kind of operatic Rapunzel

forever letting down her hair.

A "difficult" student, she fought with well-meaning mentors.
She dropped out of Julliard, married a piano prodigy brute—

he left her the night her first child was born—

and shone briefly as a soubrette in "The Merry Wives of Windsor."

None of which describes why and how talent, much less genius, fails.
"You can't know how much I want it!" she'd cry half-crocked,

and I'd rush off a money order
and not hear from her for months.

I avoid the elevator and make my way up five flights
of hospital stairs to the ICU.

D.'s awake enough to manage "—how are you?"
before she drops into a coma.

And that's about it, no commotion, no tearful goodbyes—
my eyes are unaccountably dry—and an hour later

on the leaf-strewn terrace outside
a woman approaches me; short and grim

with thin wisps of graying hair, she holds

a bouquet of pathetic looking asters,

and when I draw out a few dollars
        her withering look strikes me more

than anything has today.

"I donate these gratis, no need to thank me," she insists,
        pressing the flowers onto me, and I give them back.

MEMORY TRAIN

For weeks my mother prepares me for
    the trip to New Orleans. She tells me
about Aunt Zola, Little Buster,
    and my cousin Laura, and on the train
I already miss my mother. I sleep and read.

I keep a stack of books and postcards
    in my yellow suitcase. Now dingy shacks
appear with Negroes outside them.
    After breakfast Tennessee turns into
Alabama, blue mountains become

tar-colored fields. I push my forehead
    against the steamy glass and recall
my mother saying I'd love my
    Louisiana cousins but is this true?
The train proceeds through my childhood,

The New Orleans Zephyr, The Orange Bowl Special,
    and I peer through the window into
smoky morning light. The train rocks on,
    I like the dining car's drunken sway,
the smell of grits and bacon from the kitchen

where a black man in a white chef's hat
    flips hotcakes onto a spitting grill.
More shotgun shacks drift by: a field hand
    bends over a gunnysack, and I forget
who I belong to, who belongs to me.

The train pulls into a steamy station,
    and I give in to Aunt Zola's relentless hugs,
the stink of her Este Lauder; her car
    drifts through a junkyard of broke-down houses,
and now I sit on Zola's second story porch

on Jefferson Avenue, breathing in the stink
    of flowers I can't name, with cousins
Buster and Laura. Buster's fat as a tub.
    "Pass me the rinds," he says, and I nudge
the green avocado skin, the alligator pear,

across the table. Cousin Laura,
    two years older than me, is a thin
pony of a girl. Heat flickers over
    the canal down the block, mosquitoes bounce
fatly against the screen. Then she shows me the neat

flat skin of her belly beneath her halter,
    above her shorts, and when she lies back
in her butterfly chair, there's a hum
    as from a thousand crickets. Past four A.M.
Zola puts me to bed and I have a dream

of both my past and future. Varnished clean
    of my assumptions, tomorrow I'll forget
the hall clock striking six, a shuffle
    of a girl's feet on the stairwell, the bedroom door
creaking open and the moon caught

in my window like a fly in amber. Years
    later, all this is memory and remorse.
How time flies—I'm told it can't be measured.

Time Remembered

After Bill Evans

It rained that night and I watched moths,
mammoth-sized moths, hovering about the glowing street lamp,

        moths pregnant with street light and rain,
and I turned off the ceiling fan

and heard her singing

and it came to me that our lives together
had come and gone without me hearing her sing like that.

Gone was gone. Spring with all its attendant and inescapable suffering
was a prelude to the ruckus I heard beyond the screen.

        But still she sang, her voice altered by time and dis-
tance.

I'd like to say I heard nothing, just those moths slamming
their fleshy wings against the lamplight,

but each note rose pitch-perfect out of her like never before.

I went outside in the yard and heard a block or two away
late-night traffic on the thruway,

        and still she was there singing her brains out.

I headed down the driveway, besotted by the damp night air.

The ash and cinder of winter had blown away.

Angry low clouds were ready to drop a motherlode of rain on me.

II

FLYING LOW

In "Flying Low" Abbey Lincoln manages a series of halfsteps,
quavering between pain and pleasure as a violin
barely loud enough follows her, the words
sung so it hurts to know she means them,
and Stan Getz, a year or so from dying, plays a chorus
longer than he needs to
(he might have gone on forever)
and then Lincoln's voice soars so perfectly
just a hairbreath out-of-tune
you know the song, so dark it drags with it
a slipstream of desire, is not about Japan
(where she's written it)

       or about Miles
(who may or may not have inspired its lofty darkness)
or about how Lincoln exits the tune
with only the bass those first, final slow eight measures,

and then the piano softly behind her: nor
is it about how in Kyoto the temples at four A.M.
burnish in the halflight

       as Lincoln's taxi drives by
and a patchrobed monk looks up, lonely, from his sweeping.

CATHEDRAL OF WOOD

He stood in the narthex of the great cathedral,
aghast at the wooden angels and bestiary, the unlit
wonder of it all. No sounds this early, just blight,
gray and anesthetic, and a vague memory of a tune
they played before the crowd exited to the street.
He regarded the tulips barely up in the courtyard,
the poets and sleepy-eyed hackers quietly worshipful
in their pews, and momentarily, he forgot he wasn't Catholic—
they hadn't married in the church like she'd wanted—
and that faith was an illusion she hoped he'd maneuver
through; but all that was complicated. What he knew
weren't the gnarled carvings, the cedar staircase
festooned with saints, or his drug-riven guilt,
but last night's songs calling out to the stars.

PLAZA COLON, SANTO DOMINGO

On a side street in Santa Domingo
up from the little square
where Columbus' brother Bartolomeo
might view the conjunction of land and sea,
in the pitiless ten o'clock sun,
a couple argues over the
cost of breakfast. Below,
plastic baggies and milk cartons
churn in the slant of current,
and farther out, beyond the river's
mouth, a tanker rides the swell
into clearer water. The couple
sits in the shade, regarding
the bougainvillea. What use, Bartolomeo?
Spain, Empire, personal ambition all
falling away from you. The
morning wind must have touched you
as it touches them now, sending you
back to the indecent cool of the Alcazar
your coral sanctuary
the Oxama flowing south,
only hyacinths and gold water.

SHOOT THE PIANO PLAYER

"... smoking, drinking, never thinking of tomorrow—nonchalant"

It was always gray in Pittsburg, and their rickety house—
what a dark place with just Liz, her sad sack parents and

an out-of-tune upright piano! When drunk the old man
danced her around the living room to Fats Waller records,

her mother watching. Not long after the foundries shut down,
he collapsed of a stroke holding her in his steelworker arms.

Most dreams come from clichés like the ones she told herself
when she set off for college and met a self-proclaimed genius

named Steve who introduced her to The New Music.
As the old man predicted she flunked all her classes.

She learned to play stride & in 1969 got a gig playing piano
in a Dixie band on a student ship to Europe. It was a stormy crossing.

The boat, a revamped WW II Liberty ship, tossed the vomit-soaked
students about—the way she tells it, the Dutch captain

was sick for a week—& she caught double pneumonia.
Eventually, the band ended up in Paris. Fill in the blanks.

Steve raises his horn, pushing a hapless phrase or two down
the shiny brass tubing. But what he plays is a lie.

Shot glasses clink, the room is thick with cross-eyed cheer,
and here *she* is, plinking her brains out while "Central Park West"

goes on inside her head. You should hear Tommy Flanagan do it—
there's piano players & there's one-of-a-kind Flanagan who

reminds her of a life she might have lived had she the courage
to live it. Nights she plays piano and days she works as a script girl

for a film company in the 8th Arrondisement. She pours the bourbon,
she takes off her dress, making the boys feel at home; but Steve

never asks how her day went or where she goes after dark.
He's smug alright, smoking Davidoff cigars, spending her money,

but neither knows what they'll do when they leave Paris.
Once he came home with another woman and asked Liz to share

their bed & she didn't think a moment about doing it.
Next morning, washed clean of her presumptions, she sat

in a little garden outside Notre Dame, looking up at the gargoyles.
When she has enough money, she'll study at the Sorbonne,

she'll patronize the arts. But this life's in her blood. Rain in her face,
a barge of misfits towed upriver toward their dark gypsy future.

Tall with legs that go down to the floor, she smokes, she drinks:
the band starts up & she draws back a little. "Shoot the piano player,"

someone cries & the girls in their sequined dresses sway.
When she reaches out to touch them, they disappear.

Under Belvidere Mountain

Uncle Joe Stalin visited Vermont, July of '34,
same month and year Federico Garcia Lorca was in Eden Mills; Lorca
took two days

to sober up from a long rollicking train ride to Montpelier where Stalin
disembarked three days before:

imagine poet and tyrant passed each other in paddle boats
under Belvidere Mountain: each saw

the other's profile on the decks of lake cottages:
Stalin recovering from
delicate surgery to remove a slug
from his spine: Lorca adrift

in early summer moonshine; a trussed up Stalin
plotted terror under the stars. Lorca

sat in an ocean liner chair swatting
black flies. Then night came on, little wreaths
of cloud floated over membrane of death

a delphinium blue deep under
the murmuring mosquitoes
and transparent yellow wings.

DREAMSVILLE

Unable to sleep, he sat on the balcony to watch the traffic—
it was snowing, the city was brilliant and white—
then he wandered into the hotel bar,
bought a pack of Canadian cigarettes, and chatted up
                    the hatcheck girl who said she knew who he was.
Montreal in midwinter and the weather outside
was "frightful," but his inner parts were working.

The girl joined him for a drink at the bar. Her little feet lost
in oversize mukluks, the fringe of her camisole
revealing a half-inch scar where the cleavage began.
He had a gig a few blocks down and asked her
for another drink later, and she said she would.

Soon, he found himself alone in his hotel room.
He lay in bed and blew into his mouthpiece, warming up.
Snow spat through the balcony door,
                    night sifted around him.
He dreamed about his ex who the hatcheck girl
reminded him of, a dream that was still going on when he awoke
trailing him down the street to the club where
three mirthless Frenchmen waited for him to screw up.

Who *knows* where the soul goes if you die in a place like that?

The common language was jazz, but these men weren't playing it.
Jingle of Canadian coins, smear of lipstick on his cheek—
he heard and felt all that as he played his first notes.
                    The crowd unexpectedly cheered
as he lurched into a second chorus of a tune he'd not heard before.

The pianist smirked like a buzzard; the drummer
smashed his foot cymbal,
and he had no choice but to blunder on.
                    Then the hatcheck girl wandered in;
she loosened her hay-colored hair and the notes kept coming,
he found his stride and lost it; but he liked what the bass player
was doing, frantic runs above block piano chords,
                                    changing key a moment
with space enough for time to elude him.

Later, as he plunged his grim face into her décolleté,
she said in broken English she liked the way he played that horn,
it was "really phallic." She lay beside him draped
                    across the sheet until early next morning a wrap
at the hotel door awoke them from dreamless slumber.

EARLY AUTUMN

She'd known hours before
he'd flicked off the cassette
and told her it was over
and there was no "bottom,"
no night-storm, no puke to
mop up; a blessed change
would come, as it always did,
in the gradual unfolding,
moment to moment, of
Hodges' sax slipping into
"The Mooch" as they stood
on the deck, the air chilling
to autumn, and he'd taken
another pull on his beer—his
last before rehab—and a wolf
faced man greeted them with
undo cheer at the clinic
door: just then she thought
she heard, must have heard,
a woman sighing in the muffled
distance. But how indifferent
she felt, how evenly spread out
was her indifference as she
watched his goofy smile spasm
into tears. Then her car ride home,
        the road spitting gravel.

DEVIL'S DUES BLUES

My Spanish isn't good but I can say
"Nice weather," I can tell a man
& a kid like the devil & his son
to leave the premises.

And so when I let both in I didn't see it coming
he heaved down in my
landlady's nicest floral pattern
chair & still I didn't

give him the money, but stood in the hallway
another breathless minute,
holding the potato
just fifteen pesos,

I'd throw in an onion, he said
& the kid's eyes drifted
to the flybuzzing ceiling.
I watched the fireball

burst from the old man's mouth,
watched the curtains foul up
& the boy just laughed (in Spanish)
as the room started to burn.

Sweet potato, red Bermuda onion,
the room blazing with his hungry laughter.
More peddlers than Hell knows about
cruise the hallway. Nothing personal they say,

but I've seen their goofy
stare. He was chubby, I remember,
a little Dizzy-snoot of a beard.

And the boy had a look that said,

I've gone the limit. I know what's holy.
You know us fuckers, the boy's eyes said.
Keep us out. Don't forget
to close the door.

Lights Out on San Lazaro

(Alcoholics Anonymous was "legalized" in Cuba in 1993)

Everyone's newly sober here, their old skin dropping off,
wings freshly extended save Pablo, in his rum bucket, whose

bare feet glow in the halfdark like the feet of Lazarus.
Sunday afternoon in Havana, I listen to how Manolo woke up

one three o'clock shaking and saw the Virgin; how Ysmidra gnawed
at her knuckles till they turned blue. You tell your Mama 'bout that,

Ysmidra says, her eyes blazing righteous. I've sat half an hour,
sipping sweet water, watching Cuban baseball (Santa Clara vs.

Pinar del Rio) on a black & white TV. I've climbed three sets of
shaky stairs past stunted cilantro and red peppers in tin pots, past

slop pails and leaky latrines and dogs and cats so skinny
they aren't even scrofulous: everyone save Pablo's quit drinking.

Pablo keeps his rum under a rattan chair and takes sips
between innings. Ysmidra, his sober daughter, won't blame him

she's already had her slip and prays & goes to meetings.
Just before lights flick off a Santa Clara batter thwacks

a long drive into the Rio bleachers and a cry, irreducible & fanatic,
rises over the barrio. Who's that? (The knockknock, the cockcrow)

and Manolo sighs a long forgiving sigh. But the night's
not over lights are out, the TV's off, and in Central Havana

a siren wails ghostlike and you can hear "*No puedo vivir como asi,*" sung by some lost soul of The Revolution. The darkness

swirls, the saints' voices fill the air with such clarity
I have to stop thinking.

PERRY STREET

When war was declared, we lived in a flea-infested flat
    five blocks down from Nick's where my father
took my mom who was pregnant with me. It's a lie to say

I recall Nick's Dixieland band, but years later
    I liked to hear how I kicked Mom's tummy when
they began to play and how a tailgate trombone

marched us home through blackouts and rain.
    On weekends our Perry Street flat swarmed
with artists posing nude for each other while my father strummed

his four-string guitar. They left at four A.M. and the boozy
    shouts began; then dawn oozing over the West
Village chimney pots and Mom singing me into

an amniotic sleep. After I was born, I rode a rocking horse
    into blue oblivion, did it till I got it right, the bump & grind
of barrelhouse jazz. That's me but not me, still diapered

& barely two, gazing through whisky light onto a rain-slick
    patio, fists balled up and beyond crying. I loved B-flat,
key of the Present Moment, Key of Now. But what use, the past?

The Chianti bottle my father hid behind the stoop, Mom's
    wood shavings tossed like butts onto the floor
& the swish of her silk dress (the one with sunflowers on it)

as she carried me half-asleep down to Nick's. I went to Nick's
    before I could talk. I sat on Pee Wee Russell's lap.
I learned to jitterbug, I learned to scat.

The key to memory (and forgetting) is A-flat, the key
    of Lost Things. I'm awash tonight in a tragic
D-flat tune by—who else?—Billy Strayhorn.

The phone rings, someone sighs *Pick up, pick up.*
    The leaf-blown patio, the schnauzer that refused to bark—
these snatches of someone else's childhood are with me now.

But I can't talk, I can't answer the phone.

       The schnauzer's name was Lily.
          The bird's name was Oscar.
     Lily ate Oscar—
       I buried Oscar in a flowerpot:
     I played a dirge in D-flat.

'There's not much worth saving,' I said as they wheeled me into
       Saint Vincent's ER one night decades hence.
I put myself back together limb by broken limb,

a self reassembled, a facsimile of what I wanted
       taking shape from things that fell in pieces. Sparrows
flocked to the patio. The rain fell sweetly down.

AFTER THE LIGHTS

Years later, a Tuesday or Wednesday,
    I remember the students
out back playing tennis
    in air so cold it
puckered the rain barrel

& my radio said what it
    couldn't say while Big Joe
did bench presses in the basement
    & the radio went idiotically silent.
Remember Al Hibler

singing "After the Lights Go Down Low"?
    That's what Big Joe was crooning
when the President got shot.
    "This is all you
got to feel of it," Joe would say,

improvising. Later, a guy tries
    to pick me up in the Airliner Bar,
such bad taste I say, the street
    a sort of Moon River blue.
So I broke up with Janet

At an assassination party:
    And it was spitting snow
when I hitched through Iowa into
    oddly inaugural Illinois, no lilacs
no cortege, but for a TV's hard stare

    in the pool hall where I hustled
bus fare to New York.

MORNING WALK

Nothing like going crazy in the Deep South
which has a tradition of madmen going back
to when they beat it out of you thinking
you'd feigned it or bumbled into it
like Louis did decades ago, Louis with skin
the color of dark horse leather, his eyes
a bloody porridge of Old Testament
confusion that abated with a double
dose of Thorazine that rendered him
boringly coherent and monosyllabic.
I knew him, still know him, as we're
walkers and bump into each other
under the bug-infested palmettos
by the Confederate Cemetery
(a misnomer as most folks residing
there are former slaves or descendants
of slaves, including Louis' great-great
grand pappy). Listen close and you'll hear
those harrowing voices that have dogged him
since he ran out of meds. He walks most days
up and down, a Hammond-B playing naked
inside his head. "Everyone take that man
for granted," the neighbors say: there's always
someone poorer and crazier than you are,
they say, so maybe crazy's beside the point
and soon we'll all end up like Louis.
It's so easy, the words, the facts, pulsate
against each other, until verbs become nouns,
the adjectives are colorless
adornments on an array of lying facts.
The more I walk this neighborhood, the less
I know of my own intentions regarding
Louis, cane in hand, canvas fishing hat
sloping low on his forehead, his mouth
agape in astounded wonderment.

Moment to Moment

They were coming about, the sails luffing like crazy, and the lake
looked upside down. Oh, what to do! Would you believe
a phrase came to him now with such clarity, he had to write it down?
He thought of Shirley Horne he'd played with years ago in Brussels
singing "Once I Loved" and how, thereafter, his life had changed!
Esther's face was a knot of panic. Steer the motherfucking boat,
she shrieked, but he paid her no mind. His mind was ablaze.
Bright waves followed them aft, the wind whistled through
the scuppers. While Esther took the helm, he scribbled
the tune's chords and time signature on some foolscap he found
in the cabin. When he reemerged, the wind had dropped and the lake,
a depthless sunset blue, had calmed down. Esther still at the helm,
they cleared a headland, and now the wind recommenced with fury.
The voice of Shirley Horne, old and devastated, came back to him.
They were kilometers from port, and moment to moment their fate
and the love they shared came into question. Steer the mother-
fucking boat, he shrieked, but she paid him no mind.

Last Night at the Bayside

How far is the journey from here to a star? —George Gershwin

After the first set I went onto the splintery deck.
The three other musicians followed with drinks,

and in the early stillness a woman at the next table
carried on without letup about this and that.

I tried to tell the blind piano player what the bay
looked like at sunset, but he said after losing

his sight he didn't want reminders of what he missed.
This was our last night together, and I wanted to say

I enjoyed what he did, but he'd have none of it.
I looked over to the bass player and drummer—

they seemed clueless—and the wind had dropped,
a sailboat motored to shore and a few errant gulls

loped along the beach to where leftovers
from the day's catch were thrown into the water.

I puzzled over what the piano player felt—a wash of
sound, a flutter of invisible wings?—and on my way home,

I ran down the window and watched clouds race
across the bay. The bass player drove by, the piano

player beside him staring helplessly at the water.
Who knows why he made me uneasy? As I drove

into the hills, it began to rain, the radio from Montreal
was blowing static, a hard rain pounded down.

DEYA

It stormed a lot that summer—I'd wake
to hear the wind and rain moving up
the neighboring ridges, then I'd go out
and watch the moon kiss the mountains.
It was all Starry Night-like, the runoff
from constant rain gushing down
the clogged aqueducts, the hills lambent
with an evening's promise. I knew where
Purgatory was—a mile down the valley:
the Moors had left here eight-hundred
years ago, and little remained but snatches
of their strange music. I learned how
to drink that summer, and I partook
of the grape. I spoke the local dialect
and I read Robert Graves' "The White
Goddess" and thought about Circe and her bevy
of pigs, Circe with a tattoo of a white cloud
on her breast, her nipples fashionably pierced.
Graves claimed our village was a soul trap
and on nights like these the dead seemed
more alive than the living. What difference
did it make? The pigs snuffling roots
in the muddy courtyard, the goddess
worn out by constant fucking.

Deya, Mallorca —1970

Torch Song

Havana

I went to Yoya's and three days
drank the rum, watched the dancers
all the time a piss smell
from the back closet in the corner
while the delicate mambo,
the son & salsa swept me away.
Three days. A tumbler of sun,
pitcher of moon. But no one
hugged me, no one talked. Just listen,
Yoya said: and put her lips
into my ear and said she liked the way I sang,
the way I sat in my dress, white.
I didn't believe her I was her
demonstration piece. Smoke wreathed
around my wretched little body.

In Frankfurt

She was on a trolley headed home
to her family and it was raining
that awful industrial rain
that falls in late summer
in Frankfurt, and she was pretty
and still young with a beehive
of shellacked blonde hair, and because
she was as she'd been
back then, when I awoke it came to me
she might very well be dead,
or in a rest home, well-cared for
but nevertheless as old as I am.
It was 1959, everything was still
bombed-out and shameful in Frankfurt,
and save for me and the drummer,
our band was Jewish, Margaret
never met a Jew, so what did she know?
How well the band played and whatever
song we played made little difference
to Margaret. She said she was fatherless
and without prospects but somehow
that didn't move me. All night outside
the club, the jackhammers
were at it, rebuilding the city,
restoring the glitter

JACMEL

I slip up a stairway to where everything's
entwined and green. The balcony's festooned
with pots of anise and devil's root, basil and thyme,
the view's angelic: sunrise blanches
south Haiti's cliffs lime-green. Two girls enter
in first communion dresses, an hour
after dawn, on a nearby table a missal
pour *les enfants*, and from a church next door
more children's voices. Three days I've been here,
ignoring rumors of a coup; I watch
the sky film over like a jaundiced eye
—there'll be thunderstorms by noon.
The Madame, the *manoir's* mistress, serves me
black coffee in blue china; I sit by
the grille work and watch things change:
a gardener doesn't clip the circular
hedges; maids won't prepare my room
for guests who will not come. (Creole radio
says a strike will cripple Jacmel by noon.)
Now the girls tumble into a sea of whiteness
and the church bells ring compline. By mid-morning
I consider my options: to stay here
and in the afternoon's thyme-fragrance swing
in a wicker swing high over the rooftops
of Jacmel—or escape to Port Au Prince by van.
But the Madame's smiles, her sweet blandishments,
persuade me. "Look, I've got all these mouths to feed,"
she says. A view of seabirds, heat-ruffled garden.
Taking note, I place my key coolly
into the Madame's palm.

III

DUTCHMAN

The crew of this vessel are supposed to have been guilty of some dreadful crime and to have been stricken with pestilence ... and are ordained still to traverse the ocean on which they perished, till the period of their penance expire.

—John Leyden (1775–1811)

Down the China Sea we head toward
a Buddhist island that sits like a green duck
on the oily sea. A vagrant wind fills
the sails of our creaking ship.

I eat breakfast—fried eels, greased.
sliced turnips—while across from me
an old man spills his green tea
on his vest. The engines groan, the hull

hums its tired ah-um; there's the muscular
stench of human shit. The Dutch phrase
for "empty passion" escapes my lips.
Morning & the island's a sleepless night

away. I hear on the foredeck the helpless
scrape of an erhu—a Chinese fiddle—
the first mate wields like a fist.
It goes on & on like this.

As I step off she takes my arm & guides
me to a shop filled with souvenirs
& balms of the saved. I spend the next
three days with this woman, our hotel

room window sashed against December
wind & rain, and when we venture
out I'm surprised how white her skin is.
That's what I remember of China and

this woman. I was her "sick Dutchman."

MAYBE SEPTEMBER

Maybe September and I was in love again with
Shanghai in all its post Apocalypse splendor,
in love with an idea of a city, not the city itself.
In love with my horn & what I'd learned
those nights at the Peace Hotel. The bass player said:
shut up & hear the silences, and halfway 'round
the world, I listened to a woman from Macao
invoking the broken intervals of a steaming river,
the Buddha girls waiting for pickups on the quay.
I put down my horn and rode my bike all the way
to the old French neighborhoods. Late at night
the leaves of the camphor trees blew & scudded
along the pavement before me. I rode past the tin roof
noodle shacks, the old men in their blue caps,
an occasional fruit stand with a choice melon
sliced open like a red mouth, the clumps of
night wanderers under stage setting streetlights
and told myself I'd never been so completely happy,
never again would I feel happiness like this.

THE GREAT TRANSFORMATION

For weeks a soft rain pattered down.
No, it began: "The mind of the Great Sage

of India was intimately conveyed from west to east"
along the trade routes by lateen-sail and outrigger

                                    through the straits of Sumatra,
and decades passed
before it announced itself with
                    an ignominious rap
at a T'aoist's door.
The rain fell on the plantain leaves,
the rice paddies filled to overflowing,
and still nothing changed
in the kingdom of Han
in the court of Ch'in.
Some say the foundations were laid in the garden
of a retired bureaucrat,
others that a bird screamed in a plum tree

                        and Chinese Buddhism was born.

More poems were scribbled
as they had been for centuries
                    on damp cave walls.
A few old men walked in the rain,
their conical hats dripping wet.

THE MAN PLAYING THE TRES

Since the 1959 Cuban Revolution Yoya Gonzales has thrown
after-hours parties in her basement flat in Central Havana

The light was a narrative light,
lemon colored, shining on
our nappy heads, and the music
was a rich bolero, an umber
of guitar oil and aguardiente.

Through silk curtains came
the murmur of the *tres*.★
The man with the *tres* sat
hunched over in his felt hat

and played to the whores
and caballeros, to the attentive
listeners and slack-limbed losers,
a song, a warm bolero,

that floated, suspended, in the night's
smoky air. "Listen," the *tres* said.
"Listen." And he played *Night and Day*,
the Cole Porter tune, and Papito

pranced and dangled on an invisible beam.

★ a three-stringed banjo

HEART'S HEART & BELL ROPE

The odors are dayold barracuda, fruity gumbo; an unrefined
lowoctane stink. Mark's pounding an Irish jig on a tin marimba,

his boombox hooting sixties songs;
a Cuban couple makes love on the beach, copulating,

"fucking copulating," Mark the Mick
says. This is pure Gringo bigotry: the Spicks & Micks, the Wog

ice cream. I peg the Irishman as IRA. At the end of the quay he
rocks back and forth on the balls of his feet.

I want to go into deep
dark, he says, to sift what's indecent dark

from these Indies, these cryptic margins.
A Havana cop glimpses where the Irishman's

been before lights blinked off down the esplanade.
Somebody's lit up to his ears, doing with gusto what's left of this town.

Under the embargoed stars, I pray for the littered
shingle, the keys and islets from here to Bandolero,

and I pray for the couple who squirm like fish, humping
their hunger away. Back in the Hotel Escaleras

I drift into a sailor's quirky sleep;
I dream a Russian wedding, shot glasses filled with

ambassadorially clear vodka; and when I awake
it's three A.M.. Havana's still and grim. The room's

awash in aquamarine. Somewhere, a bell's tinkling; a rope hangs down,
looped, like a bellrope, to the city's spasming heart.

Love among the Cannibals

The start of a blistering Tampa summer and my skin
was blood-orange, my eyes hep-yellow due to the Klonopin.
A woman from rehab paid for my trip down—
            she'd financed the clinic—but my legs ached from
a night of long prayer. I was pitiful but eager
to play later that week with a guy I knew
from Mykonos the year before. Tom had been sober, me too,
and oh, the stories we could tell! We took to a woman we'd met
            at a café where we played in town—we loved
the loose careless way she carried on.

Looking down the Bougainville-draped veranda,
playing tunes of the old masters, George Gershwin, Harold Arlen
(What's in a song but a pathway into another era?)
we congratulated ourselves on being
clean and sober all these months. The music went on—
there's long gaps each day I can't account for—
            and I began to resent how we'd squandered
our talent, the woman we both loved
in shabby Fellini-like dishabille,
the notes we played drifting like smoke from grass fires
raging all Spring on Delos, and a kind of brilliance,
came between us.

A few Lenten weeks before Easter,
Tom took the boat to Athens under a sky so impermeably blue
I doubted my senses. The day carried on like it always did,
the piano still there out of tune, sheet music under the seat,
            and I was overcome by my past and my place in it.
The girl turned out to be a thief, she stole a wristwatch,
a box of Dominican cigars, and her poverty endeared her to me.
But those tunes, lovely signature tunes,

still go to my head. I stood on the overgrown walkway,
broken windows, scent of limes—and without warning
night fell. I saw through a break in the foliage
the girl mounting the garden stairs. Up in the scoured
mountains rose the moon, sweet and wild.

BORDER CROSSING

He'd taken some kind of awful drug the hatcheck girl
had given him and halfway through the first set the next night
things didn't add up, the other cats started looking like cats,
and so on. This wasn't the '60's and he was no longer his blazing
former self but had reverted to the regimen of the ancestors—
snifter of schnapps for breakfast, a cocktail before noon,
and now that drug she had given him. Nothing distinguished
this bar from any other but its name, Green Dolphin Street
the band had dubbed Purple Porpoise Alley, ha-ha.
"Take me home with you," she said after the gig, but
he had no home to go to. Beyond the outbuildings bulrushes
sighed and rustled in the rain, and more distant, the glow
of the meat packing plants of Cote Saint Luke and
the great Iron Fist of The North where all journeys end.

The hatcheck girl had a car, so they headed south,
his horn strapped like a corpse to the roof. At midnight
when they approached the border, lightning flickered
along the Richelieu and the customs station was brightly lit
to catch any crime. As they crossed the river bridge, a monkey—
yes, a monkey!—scrambled from the bushes in flight
from here to there, my God a monkey in these latitudes,
and when he told the border guard (who wasn't impressed)
he and the hatcheck girl were made to get out of the car.

The border guard was tall with the bulging eyes of Cerebus
who guards the gates of the Underworld to prevent those who
have crossed the river Styx from ever escaping. Thence,
the ritual humiliations sidemen suffer that haven't
made a name for themselves. As he took his horn down
from the roof of the car, he realized in horror what

that drug was the girl had given him. He washed away that
thought as he removed his trombone from its tattered case.
What a beautiful horn it was, a tarnished and dented King,
and he brought the mouthpiece to his lips. Thence
followed the years of exile in dives across Quebec,
the frozen wastes of La Belle Province.

To Mike Martello
on His Eighty-Eighth Birthday

An ordinary night at The Bayside,
      just a tremble of a breeze
in the licks Mike plays on his guitar,
a couple of local girls dancing together
      in the half-light, but what's
the song, the number?

"Just like a flame," Mike hums,
      "love burned brightly then became
empty smoke," while the bass player
lays out a cluster of unamplified notes
      that last until the final chorus.
An oyster shell moon rises

above the anchorage and the tune's
      "Gone with the Wind," but goddamn, Mike,
you're anything but gone, you'll be
around until the wrecking ball
      of midnight descends on all of us.

HEAD WOUND

It's noon halfway through our last century
in a dimly lit reading room outside Paris
and the blinds are half-drawn against the glare—
though there's no glare: at times it's rainy,
then the June day gives way to sun-swept
snowbells whose reflections shimmer and wobble
against the pane. A white-gloved librarian
sets the duke's daybook on a scarred oak table.
The antiseptic cell should spark contemplation
but doesn't. (Your mind's awhirl.) You're given
white gloves, a magnifying glass, and after
a quick check of the timetable back to Paris,
you leaf through the vellum pages, squinting
at landscapes alive with carnelian reds
and nectarines—Lord, it's *all so* helplessly
beautiful that you lean back to anchor yourself.
The *Tres Riches Heures*, a calendar book,
was made to fit into The Duke de Berry's
ample pocket. The sky in each miniature's
a startling eggshell blue. Gilded zodiac
symbols over-arch each page—and somehow
it all coheres: northern France in smoky ruins,
The Hundred Years War having emptied
the duke's coffers—and so this dream of
crenellated castles, streams wandering
nowhere, and girls so lovely they float
a few feet off the ground. An hour or two
passes at the Musee Conde on the banks
of the slow-moving Oise not far from where
Van Gogh shot himself. Wars were fought
and lives lost here, none less precious than yours
that was saved by your infantryman's helmet.
Since then you've been cursed by migraines, tunnel vision,

but these paintings—so much detail's been casually
left out, shadows for one thing, (who back then
knew where the light came from?) and the moon.
Before the War, you chose life as a musician—
it's ruined *you* twice over—and you know
what the spaces between notes mean.
The ancient Chinese knew this too as did
your artist mother who, when you were ten,
showed you the *Tres Riches Heures*. She hoped
you'd take up painting, but you've no talent:
between gigs you visit the Louvre and read Proust.
"How *cosmopolitan!*" *she* writes, enclosing
with her note a check for next month's rent—
the poor woman knows you're not right, you've got
a head wound that will not heal. The Limbourgs,
Herman, Paul and Johan, traveled from
the Low Country to paint for Phillip the Bold,
King of France, brother of the Duke who after
Phillip's death hired them to illustrate
the Bible and this little book.
You woke this morning in a room two floors up
from yours to the ruin of hangover
and took the Metro to Neuilly
and another train to Chantilly
where you pore page after page over
the *Tres Riches Heures of the Duke de Berry.*
You know little of Medieval History,
less about the Duke who suffered,
like you, from migraine and spent
his patrimony on art. Nearing
the end of his days he didn't care.
You turn to the month of December—
a boar hunt in muddy dun colors
and cinnabar reds. The dogs plunge
into the boar's haunches. A broadfaced man
grapples with a tangle of dogs

and holds back a bloodhound whose tongue
lolls from his mouth like a red flag.
The suppleness of the dogs, the way their bodies
contract and ripple—each finds a haunch,
a loin, to gnaw on. And as for the men,
they're not worth much more to the Limbourgs
than a few centimes in the hands of the poor.
But they are men, alive to how the leaves
rattle in the wind and alert to when
the dogs catch a scent and begin their
feverish baying. The trees are stained
in pale russets, December light streaks
the forest floor, stunning you to silence.
The hunters' bellies rumble with cold
porridge, their armpits exude an angry stench.
Once they were held by mothers who caressed them,
who asked a priest to bless them, and sent them
into this world. Look how life has changed them!
As you exit into late-June sunlight you think
of your own mother and the gig you played
the night before. Thanks to her she's left you
countless ways to see through migraine a world
transformed, fish to bird, bicuspid to crab,
snakes into the flaming bell of your horn.
You walk back to town toward the depot,
past a burnt out tank, its monster treads half-buried
in mud, and you slip into a moment
when time stopped and a fly floated, suspended,
in midair. *Your head wound's caused your migraine
and your loss of perfect pitch—a bullet
to the brain will do that,* the doctors joke.
This café on a hillcrest above the Oise
seems a nice place to stop. A girl brings
your first carafe. The poplars are greening out,
the hills of Picardy are burnt umber.
It won't be long till you get your vision back.

SEEING YOUR FACE

Suddenly jazz got a bad
name. I gave the future
smooches goodbye. Goodbye
Pop, goodbye everything forgivable:
I didn't tell you
though I thought I should
how the world
tilted into oily darkness
when my father came in
singing from the hall.
"Music," he said, "I
like that." And how that
hairbrush burned, how
the music swelled up loud.
Loud, he said.
And for years.
And so for years.
And when I met you,
and you asked, "You like
jazz music?" and your fingers
shook like mine did,
when each syllable congealed
into a love that seemed un–
breakable, I knew, I knew.
It's like I was there,
grinning into your
face, like I'm with you now.

THE PEACOCKS

For Jimmy Rowles

"After a fortnight's work Caravaggio will swagger about for a month or two with a sword at his side and a servant following him, from one ballcourt to the next, ever ready to engage in a fight or an argument."

A late-August afternoon and the dahlias
are still in bloom, the Swiss painters
are at their easels waiting for the sun
to go down. I spend an hour or two
watching the peacocks strut across
the lawn, tattered, unkempt has-been
peacocks, in full-molt, fallen on hard times.
A rubble of second-class beach
between Ischia and Naples, and Chet's
at the cabana bar, touching the spot
where last night the girl nipped him. One more
shot and a beer and my thoughts shunt back
to the strung-out Florentine who died
of a head-wound not far from here.
That larcenous smile, that junky stare.
Chet's almost a dead ringer for
Caravaggio: everyone knew
his assassin was a parvenu,
a rank amateur. Before the final blow,
butterflies flitted across his cornea,
he saw through dying light the green sea
& these islands dark as ripe plums.
The afternoon wears on. Chet tries out
a few girly notes on his beat-up trumpet;
a pair of hang-gliders drifts seaward
over the tawny land. Late-August's sadness
is like no other—everything's half-gone,

half-used-up and recumbently sad,
like the saints Caravaggio painted
are sad. Someone shooed away the gulls,
scraped off the zinc-whites, the oceanic greens,
and someone raked through the sand and found
a florin or two. Caravaggio's blood darkened
into allegory. What *about*
poor Caravaggio? There were his
aberrations—his unpaid card-debts,
a predilection for unprotected sex,
and a lot of violence; they rifled
his pockets, cut the Medici ring from
his thumb—and now the evening gives way
to the first few bitter notes from
Chet's horn. The peacocks circle the bar,
alert for handouts. Lights quiver and blink
across the amphitheater of the bay,
and he lifts a wobbly finger at the girl
who's so lovely she wears your eyes out.
Can anyone spare, she asks, a few lira
for the trip back to Naples?

To Daniel Whedon

aka Omni, Graffiti Artist

Does it matter he pissed his early life
away signing his name with the swift urgency
only the old masters matched on plaster?
Once applied, the paint took a few transient
moments to dry. Hunched or crouched
between railroad ties, keyed into
the Third Rail's threat inches away,
only a headlamp's arc walled him off
from oblivion. Call this *Art Al Fresco*,
of paint and fixative dripping into
a gangland squint—an image
he'd keep with him the rest of his days.
No pope or prince patronized his art,
no one cried "Hark!" as the BMT
skanked off into midtown darkness.

IV

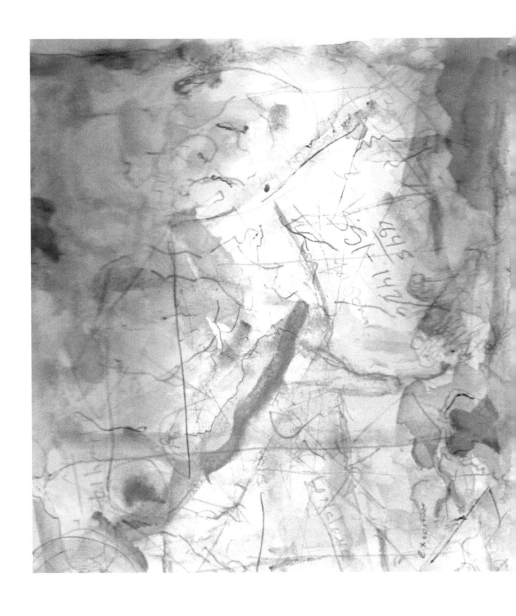

WHAT MATTERS

for Charles Wright

Tonight Alice sang the story of her life, her voice with a mouthful
of love in it. Alice's got bad teeth. Bad teeth don't help you sing better,
but she's endowed with a perfect memory of the road.
I used to think all forms of landscape were biographical,
                    and driving home it's still nice to believe
that's true! The sky clears. I turn off Sports Radio
and belt out a midnight aria for anyone who'll hear—
and nobody, thank goodness, does. I put my horn down
an hour ago and said to Alice, looking at her best self
in the barroom mirror, "Alice, you sing like
somebody I know," and hiding her smile, she said,
"How nice for you to say that.
                    But whom do I remind you of? And where'd
you get that nice silk shirt?" Touching the loose pink fabric.
I downed another frosty O'douls. "The band just wants you
to sing a tune, what else matters?" I said,
and she sang "That Old Devil Moon" which I totally
relate to now squinting down the lonely Georgia highway.
                    Sonny Stitt used to say, "If you want to play drunk,
you gotta practice drunk," which reminds me how
untrue I've been to my finest impulses. I pass a cattle truck
heading north, like me, toward Savannah, and I feel light and fragrant,
at one with moon and marshland, full of a love for jazz and Alice,
an oceanic love our mothers told us to be suspicious of.

Cemeterio Colon

The spot's simple: a white coffin, pesos
collected in a tin cup. Emilia's statue

stands at an angle to her tomb,
hair tousled, an infant in her arms:

behind her stand her rivals—celestially white,
grave upon grave, a few penitents—

a plump guide whose smile dazzles, and her
scrofulous dog tied at tomb-side; she wears

white pumps, an unassuming pink sweater,
and says,—her face half-crazed—"Emilia

gave up her life for love"; so Maria gives
herself this morning to the resurrection.

At the University of Havana she taught
the pre-Raphaelites; like Emilia, she

had a lover—a student with thick
Rosseti-ish hair, eyes like the Black Madonna's,

a little man with small, smooth hands. In short,
Maria says she loved him and lost him

in the upshot of a scandal—and left him
for her job; in the weeks following

their separation she fell into an *obscuridad* —
and now nothing redeems her save visits to

Emilia's grave. A child placed beneath
her mother's legs. The body exhumed

years later. The nameless child had climbed
into Emilia's arms—not so much

a miracle as a puzzle, I say,
and Maria shrugs me off—Look, I'm sane,

she says and shows me her hands—they do not
tremble. Each penitent touches

Emilia's gown's smooth folds, kisses
the infant's smooth stone head, retires to the shade:

each tomb along the way exhibits
its own sweetness—marble heaped on marbled,

winged stallions, and saints—boulevards of saints.
Imagine Emilia's husband dressed

in a silk suit, cigar in hand, genuflecting
before these effigies; imagine

those sweet angels, that fin-de-siecle drama
in an effulgence of white flowers—

dead mother with dead child in her arms.

While Fishing on Cathead Creek, a Woman's Face Floats Up from the Weeds and Accuses Me

And reluctantly
I watch the ratty trail of leaves
the gator idling in a slough

a mockingbird
flickering along hedgy tree-
tops

while in Paris, a woman who's
paid by a judge
to let him admonish her
        leans
carelessly across his bed

staring out the window
into the afternoon—
the little orange cars flaming
in the street—till

he's through and they can be seen

among pedestrians carrying
their bread through
     rain

bundled like everyone into drabness
a pleasant

alternative, she thinks,
to eating in the dive
where students quarrel

in a French so strident
it might well be

another language:

thirty years later through a shimmer
of memory, she crumples her napkin

regards

me so intently

I cannot finish whatever I'm thinking.

I hate being poor,

She still seems to say
her voice unforgivable
and clear while

I cast my line on the water's smudged green
surface, evening now,

the last light draining
into Low Country darkness

and taste the cabbage soup,
the hard bread

sopped in steamy juices

listening to her story

as though it were me
hurrying up five flights

on Rue Jean d'Arc,
opening the door to a flat
that reveals a view of such meanness

that I must turn abruptly away.

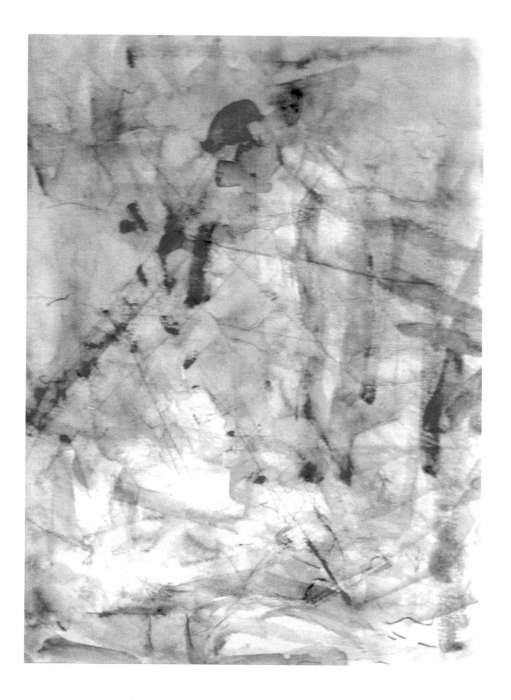

Afternoon Intermezzo

November and for three weeks there's been no more than a spatter of
    rain.

The sprinklers are at it spraying joy all around and the striped bass
    fishermen
are out catching the last sun—Good Lord, the day's so nice

I'm tempted to give away my old Bill Evans records.

But I don't.

I find my way in the balmy weather down to Sheila's
Presbyterian Thrift Shop where an etching by an unknown

(by me) Portuguese artist catches my eye.

At $40 it might be a steal. Despite the weather,
Sheila who suffers from vertigo and is heavily medicated,

has no interest in my Bill Evans records.

Lucky me!

I buy the print and carry it home where it now hangs above
where the piano should be, and at half-past four

I'm standing in the door listening
to Bill Evans' few spare arpeggios bloom

and fade into the afternoon.

Down at the wharf the striped bass fishermen
have disembarked, but I can't reproduce this peaceful scene:

a blue heron stands in the weeds so close
he might hear me breathing.

Parisian Thoroughfare

Don't know how we got that gig that summer
nor do I recall clearly the boys in our band—
and we *were* boys back then, planning a grand life around music.
I was nineteen, my growth already stunted:
I wandered the Latin Quarter, went to the *Jeu de Pomme*
in the afternoons to commune with the Impressionists.
　　　　Once I saw Bud Powell in a Montparnasse bistro,
and though I was too drunk to hear what he was playing,
I saw in his empty stare the look of genius. Puking my eyes out
in the Luxembourg Gardens, smoking my first
reefer with a Moroccan woman years
older than me and so beautiful I thought
　　　　　　she might break—that's what I remember
from back then. She asked me to her place,
no strings attached, where everything was white—
white baby grand, white shag carpet—and we ate
on the floor with our hands.

I played better that summer than I should have,
that kept me in the mix. I didn't take solitary
walks or frequent the brothels; a scrap of
scribbled sheet music that couldn't find the trash,
the after-work girls smiling up from a bench on the Ilse-St. Louis,
　　　　or those agonizing ten blocks she dragged me to
the American Hospital with a gash
that ran from my mouth to my bloody chin,
I can't say any of that, even the woman and her kindness,
and the standards we played that sweltering August,
brings me peace now. A decade later, I moved back to Paris
sober, a sports jacket and a pair of slacks richer.
By then the jazz clubs had closed. The street where I lived

was called Rue Jeanne d'Arc—up the hill the market
and down two blocks the Metro.

I no longer believed I was gifted, but looked
forward to the view of slate-roof houses, a workingclass quarter.
As the cab driver went on in his impossible French,
cursing the traffic, wheeling past one little disaster after another,
I reminded myself I'd led an interesting, an eventful life.
       Bud Powell's music, the frenzy he played it in, the impossibility
of getting it right, explains why he went crazy.
He tried to escape the rule of the left hand
and played the piano like a horn.
I heard it back then, what was absent, the notes
he left out. To my untrained ear, these seemed
like mistakes. I hear on the Blue Note records
Powell's false starts, his heroic retakes,
his breath coming fast, as if I were
at the Montparnasse bar with him.

Casa Fortunada: Museum of Fallen Objects

The Contessa rearranges her porcelain—
Dresden dolls and Wedgewoods,

grapefruit spoons and pale letter openers,
and more porcelain, everything perfectly Late Eighteenth Century —

and swirls into her sitting room and sees a table laid for invisible guests,
china glittering, sardine forks basking

                    in a light that loves to shine,

when a shutter is forced open to let in more sunlight
to illumine a grand piano she hears

beyond the unruly garden.

Nothing stirs save the Contessa and her lover's shadow
lost in music they were dancing to when Fidel entered Havana;

                    she recalls the Cole Porter tune Benny More
was singing, and how he leaned with sartorial ease

into his microphone, how the rose-petal girls scattered

onto the torch-lit terrace and an arpeggio of
machine gun fire smashed the ceiling-high French windows.

The more reality takes shape, the more it loses intensity—
that's the insane thought that took hold

                    those weeks after he was wrenched
from her arms and shot in the beach sand

outside the Copacabana. Blood spattered onto
the terrified dancefloor, a smatter

of blood staining her low-cut chiffon dress.
    The wind rustles the curtains now and dies away.

But she has no clock, only dust and decay
to measure her age, her ruination.

After Dark

For weeks after surgery,
I wondered if I'd play again.
My horn stood in a corner,
its tarnished bell gathering
dust, and when the desire came
over me, I went out to make
a fool of myself again. Down
Jackson Street, tunes, fragments
of tunes, trailed behind me,
lifting off to wherever notes go
after dark. Jelly Roll Morton,
grinning his diamond-studded grin,
famously said, "Get up from
that piano, you hurtin' its feelings—"
and there was some truth in that.
To my south, my world fell away
to ducks on the water, geese
on the water, a woman with rain-
straight hair casting from shore
for whatever came by. The air
filled with a burnt stink of
barbeque, the neighborhood
turned from black to white,
and I kept walking, caught
in the solitude of a life
I'd so haphazardly lived.

THE DEATH OF RUSS COLUMBO

I don't recall the plane, but I remember
the cab trip out from Palma to Fornalutch (or lux),
cruising with a surly hack the tortuous cordillera
that walls off the west of the island.
I was witty, I was drunk,
and Don, embarrassed, sent me to the kitchen

    with sons Dino and Chuck. I flew
all the way from Madrid for this! Off
the hootch three months, in a moment's fancy
on Madrid's *gran via*, I'd had my first brandy,
sat back, watched the girls in their maxis and calf-

    skin jackets. On Don's terrace ex-patriot
anomie. The royal blues of Don's blue blazer
bleed into sullen backdrops
of sea and olive orchards. The world's terra-cotta. I
look vaguely Etruscan. A copy of *Homage to Catalonia*
lies on the toilet top, page-marked

by a sapphire tie-clasp. Returning to the terrace,
I note I'm not the guest of honor; the voice of Russ
Columbo—somehow distantly related to Don —
croons through verdant lattice, white Moorish,
mint tea afternoon (with complimentary
clarinet obligato) and I'm suddenly twisted

    like a churro into the memory of Columbo's funeral,
the gardenias brought by Loretta Young, the Boswall sisters
serving vino, spaghetti. At the wake, Jimmy McPartland
played Columbo's signature tune, "Prisoner of Love": reading
    the record
jacket, I see the name Lansing something, the singer's

friend and photographer who'd shot him with a pearl
handled dueling pistol that doubled as a cigarette lighter.
"C'mon, c'mon." Don sees me
on the terrace, glass of *vino* and *sifon* in one hand.
The guests have left, only Don, Dino and Chuck sweeping
party refuse, and me facing the roofs

      and campaniles of Fornalutch. One voluptuary star blooms
above the village, and over days my new
life tapers to beer at noon, cafes on Palma's
Paseo Generalissimo, but mostly Fornalutch.
For three weeks I've been aware of alcohol's slow accretion:
once I was holding two drinks.

Don poured me one, I made another, while he rummaged
in old clippings, showed me a 1955 Times squibb
proclaiming him inventor of artificial snow. Like me,
he says, his best years are behind him.
Chopin, I remember, lived in Valdemossa

      with George Sand; Sand's daughter, wearing pants, was
thought strange by locals, was lonely as Chopin, who died
during the Mallorcan winter. But on a fair day in late summer,
sun falling like rain on red pantiles, the high bluffs
visible and unblushingly green, in liquid per-

emptory clarity, it all seems strange; Columbo croons
from the sitting room, and one hears music—the scratchy
metallurgy of early RCA—as though it were painted
on lemons that bob in afternoon breeze. Over *creme de menthe*,
my pernod—a momentary calm. "It's disconcerting to

      have you show up," Don says. "There was no one to call."
I tell him about my dream: a ghost ship sails into Palma's
harbor, lanyards clinking against the odd fitting.
A trolley trends toward el puerto; murmuring cypress,

an occasional coughing Lambretta...and if I stand by
the patio window, Colombo's voice glances off stone wall, plaza
        tile,

like a ricocheting bullet—the *pistola* cigarette
lighter went off as Lance lit Russ's Camel—and the photographer
mourned The record jacket goes on: 1935 in rainy LA, Lance
        jay-
walked Sunset Strip, heading for one bar or another,
was struck from behind—two years after Russ's death –
and hurried to Hollywood Hospital. Later he told
        Loretta how in his delirium Russ stood at the end
of a misty corridor, dressed in white, motioning, "C'mon,
c'mon." Colombo's smile was rapturous. Lance had never been
so completely happy and I think of what-
ever it was brought us here, the way Russ was, playing violin

in Bing's Band, working to get the sound right. I move out-
side (the town looks pinched into pastels). "Too much
rapidity in our veins," Don says, trying to cool us down.
"Atoms disintegrating at a predictable rate, it's
time speeding up toward the end of the century." And
across our valley, a breeze ruffles the tops

        of trees. Gulls slide down planes of wind, slanting

                                                wingtips
toward the water.

THE WILMORES

The Reverend Wilmore's wife
wears nun-like blues, a white
African Methodist kerchief, sits
in a mahogany rocking chair,
fingers splayed out on her thighs;
the Dominican sky's scrawled over
with thunderheads. The wind
worries the corners of her kerchief,
rattles the half-drawn shutters.
I hear in her clear plantation
speech the accents—the slurred
consonants—of my mother, *her*
story no less believable —
both are true—while above
the the barrio her granddaughter
Tereza stutters into an English
she half-remembers. Her hair
is *amarillo*, her skin the color
of a darkened peach. We sit later
with Tereza. Roofholes leak in
oblong light, sweat rivets
Tereza's forehead. She wears a
"Go Mets" T-shirt, torn shorts,
her house less commodious
than her grandmother's: two chairs,
moldering, broken floorboards;
no use, she says fixing things up
as new cinderblock affairs
will replace what's left of these
charming slum houses next year
or the year after. The view
is lovely first, then one sees

the open sewer, the sign:
"Bienvenidos al Bronx." Down
the churning arroyo palms rise,
a choking wind blows. Tereza's
pet pig shuffles a pail
of slops outside the door.

Samana, The Dominican Republic, 1987

OUR LADY OF PERPETUAL SNOWS

Esther, the hatcheck girl, found them a little flat in town,

and he liked the rough honest company of men and women
                    with whom he had little in common;
he liked, too, the North Country bands

that played tunes he hadn't heard in years. It was all a challenge—
the late night drives with Esther down lonely snow-filled roads,

the impossible language only a native could understand.
But tonight on the first set the guitar player managed just a chorus

or two before things fell apart and he lost the beat, one chord
elbowed furiously into another, the notes blowing out of his head

were hard to take. He was done with this genius: in the third bar
he'd wanted an F-major chord, but what came out was a shriek.

The bass player drew out a handgun and aimed it at the guitarist's head.
How would this end? *Mon Dieu*, Play the fucking chord, as written,

he shouted, but the guitar player ignored him. Beyond the stripper cage,
Esther was chatting up a pair of Mohawks from the casino nearby.

Again—time to flee. They drove for miles, Esther beside him,
assaulted by an army of stars. He knew a pianist who'd taken orders

at a Benedictine monastery nearby. He told Esther the monks somehow
managed to grow grapes that gained their savor from the terrible cold.

The Monastery sat poised on a cliff above a frozen lake.
They entered through its damp portal to find his friend in a little cell

eye-level with the lake. Years of devoted lacerations had done him no
   good.
(Eternality was not much sought after in this icebox.)

and he lived on a boundary beyond sin and redemption
the monks told him was Purgatory. He'd taken vows of silence,

but never a talker he'd said all he needed to say.
Next morning, at Matins, his friend—call him Gerald—

accompanied the monks' chanting on a Hammond-B organ.
(Imagine a Hammond-B in that cold drafty place!)

He and Esther sat in reverential silence, the monk's voices
rising to the bat-filled rafters, a look of rapture transforming

Gerald's formerly drug-ravaged face. The monks—
they were so aged & feeble most entered the chapel on crutches—

looked transformed by Gerald wailing away on the Hammond-B.
He glanced at Esther huddled like a little Pocahontas beside him,

and again he felt the joy bred from their ceaseless wandering.
They watched the monks hobble single-file out from the chapel,

their sweet voices still resounding in their heathen hearts.
Where to, now? Outside, a wind was raging, the frozen lake

had vanished in the blinding snow. Next morning Bach,
or the ghost of Johann Sebastian, was playing the Hammond B

down the hall. Esther said everything seemed to ripple
in time with it—the lake, the darkened houses of a town

they'd driven through on their way to the monastery: first the blouse, then the flag of her dignity she hastily tore off—these things

drew him to her, but in their cold, musty bed it got complicated.
Her nipples hardening in the unearthly cold, the needy look

she gave him as she ran her hand up his thigh—because
of his own need he noticed none of this. He heard Gerald stride

into Bach's Toccata and Fugue and he came brightly inside her.
All stops were out now, they were on a fast-track to damnation.

But a little light at the end of the ecclesiastical tunnel,
a little heat not strictly from Hell. Nothing lasts and lasts,

the Buddhist say, and there's some truth in this.
A wan northern light buttered the planks of their Spartan cell.

City of Light

We saw up ahead
our disappointment
a narrow street,
more a crack in the city walls than
a corridor, a little light
falling from a grid of windows,
and I knew it was, had to be,
morning from how the alley, or corridor,
opened onto a little town,
and a few dusty vendors,
a lake of light falling softly
across the faces of
shop keepers; and we heard the music,
out of the irrevocable past, heard
it carry along
the esplanade, drifting
toward the surf and out to sea.

EMBARKATION

Beyond the dock, a lonely scow puts out for
  a day's crabbing. Mist in the saw grass,
the palmettos, a breath of air that carries me
south into a lost heathen world.
  I love being Black, I love being white too!
According to legend, I should be dead by now,
but I'm still alive, the pious descendant of
  some tone-deaf rice plantation ancestor
who didn't know the difference between
a cakewalk and a ramble. Oh, we interbred,
  we miscegenated! "Stop the music,"
somebody shouts, "Let's take it from the top!"
and I swoon, I tremble, into a tune so fresh,
  so new, I've left the other cats behind.
When I'm done, the sky darkens with evening clouds.
The chords I effortlessly lay down—
  the clash of a foot cymbal, the rattle
of a washtub bass—spirit me back
to the sadness I felt when I first heard
  church music. The river's alive with gulls
and plover, the band's packed up and ready
  to go home. Useless to anyone but myself,
I'm drunk in the ruins of God's Creation.

BACK STREET

Walking down Backstreet
to Cathead Creek this A.M.,
little black girl in yellow shorts
followed by a fierce-looking dog
rides up her bike to me & says,
"Basil don't mean no harm to nobody."
Off in the Georgia woods a rooster
crows, another crows back across
the street. Little girl says, "Them's
trained chickens, you say jump
& all five of them jump, you say
lie down and they lie down. But
I don't go back in there, big
wolf dawg about eat me up, there's
all kinds of animals. You know
I got cats, thirteen, they all fixed."
Then—a brilliant smile: "Well, nice
to meet you," and she rides off.
And so it goes. I'm planting
a gardenia bush today

TONY WHEDON is the author of the poetry books *Things to Pray to in Vermont* Press and *The Falklands Quartet*, and the poetry chapbook *The Tres Riches Heures*. His poems and essays appear in *Harpers, American Poetry Review, Iowa Review, Prairie Schooner, Sewanee Review, Ploughshares* and over a hundred other literary magazines. His essay collection *A Language Dark Enough: Essays on Exile* won the *Mid-List* Press award for Creative Nonfiction. Tony is a working trombone player and the leader of the poetry/jazz ensemble PoJazz. Along with Neil Shepard, he founded *Green Mountains Review*. He lives with his wife Suzanne in Montgomery, Vermont.